Hanukkah
for
Jesus Followers

by

Tracy Krauss

Fictitious Ink Publishing
Tumbler Ridge, BC

Published by **Fictitious Ink Publishing**, Tumbler Ridge, BC, Canada, V0C 2W0

FOREWORD

Why celebrate Hanukkah as a Christian? Isn't it a Jewish holiday?

Of course, the answer to the second question is, "Yes, it is a Jewish holiday." But that still leaves us to ponder the "Why?"

In Romans 11, Paul goes into detail about how we, as Christians, have been "grafted in" to the root.

"If some of the branches have been broken off, and you, though a wild olive shoot, have been grafted in among the others and now share in the nourishing sap from the olive root..." Romans 11; 17 (NIV)

We have an inheritance along with our Jewish brothers and sisters and can partake of all the good gifts God has for us, which includes celebrations such as Hanukkah! What a rich heritage! Why *not* celebrate?

It is my prayer that you will have fun and be inspired during this holiday season.

INTRODUCTION

What Is The Feast of Dedication?

The *Feast of Dedication*, better known as Hanukkah, takes place each year at the end of the Jewish month of "Kislev" and goes into the beginning of the next month, "Tevet". While most Christians won't need to remember that bit of detail, (or may not even care!) it is interesting to note that Jesus celebrated Hanukkah, even though it is not listed with the other holy feasts laid out in the law.

The word 'Hanukkah' can be translated as 'Dedication', because the celebration marked a time when Jews re-dedicated the temple and themselves to the Lord.

Both Hanukkah and Christmas include a tradition of gift giving. Unfortunately, materialism and even greed have crept into modern day holiday festivities. It's a wonderful time to reflect on the importance of sacrificial giving since it shouldn't be about the size of the gift or the money spent. It is about a heart that is pure before God and wants to bless others. Although God's promise of blessings for those who are generous should not be the reason for giving, it is an outcome that we can look forward to as we give generously this season.

Scripture:

Acts 20: 35

In everything I did, I showed you that by this kind of hard work we must help the weak, remembering the words the Lord Jesus himself said: "It is more blessed to give than to receive." (NIV)

Luke 12: 32–34

Fear not, little flock, for it is your Father's good pleasure to give you the kingdom. Sell your possessions, and give to the needy. Provide yourselves with moneybags that do not grow old, with a treasure in the heavens that does not fail, where no thief approaches and no moth destroys. For where your treasure is, there will your heart be also. (ESV)

Mark 12: 41–44

And He sat down opposite the treasury and watched the people putting money into the offering box. Many rich people put in large sums. And a poor widow came and put in two small copper coins, which make a penny. And He called His disciples to Him and said to them, "Truly, I say to you, this poor widow has put in more than all those who are contributing to the offering box. For they all contributed out of their abundance, but she out of her poverty has put in everything she had, all she had to live on." (ESV)

2 Corinthians 9: 6–11

The point is this: whoever sows sparingly will also reap sparingly, and whoever sows bountifully will also reap bountifully. Each one must give as he has decided in his heart, not reluctantly or under compulsion, for God loves a cheerful giver. And God is able to make all grace abound to you, so that having all sufficiency in all things at all times, you may abound in every good work. As it is written,

"He has distributed freely, He has given to the poor; His righteousness endures forever."

He who supplies seed to the sower and bread for food will supply and multiply your seed for sowing and increase the harvest of your righteousness. You will be enriched in every way to be generous in every way, which through us will produce thanksgiving to God. (ESV)

Psalm 112: 5

Good will come to those who are generous and lend freely, who conduct their affairs with justice. (ESV)

Proverbs 11: 25

A generous person will prosper; whoever refreshes others will be refreshed. (NIV)

Prayer focus:

Thank You for the extravagance of Your love and faithfulness, Lord. Even without counting my material blessings, which are abundant compared to many others around the world, You have blessed me beyond measure. Help me to be a generous and cheerful giver, not just during the holiday season, but all year long.

Ḥanukkah Eve

On this night, one candle is lit on a nine branched menorah, or candelabra. (Different from the traditional menorah which only has seven branches.) Even though this celebration was not instituted in the law, Jesus celebrated it, as evidenced in the book of John.

In today's scripture, Jesus reminds us that nothing can snatch us out of His hand. What a wonderful promise to those who believe! Traditionally, a prayer of blessing is recited at the lighting of the candles which goes as follows:

"Blessed are You, Oh Lord our God, King of the Universe, who has set us apart by Your commandments and commanded us to kindle the lights of Hanukkah. Blessed are You Oh Lord our God, King of the universe, who has done miracles for our fathers in the days at this season. Blessed are You Oh Lord our God, King of the universe, who has kept us in life, sustaining us, and who has brought us to this season."

Scripture:
John 10: 22–30

Then came the Festival of Dedication at Jerusalem. It was winter, and Jesus was in the temple courts walking in Solomon's Colonnade. The Jews who were there gathered around Him, saying, "How long will you keep us in suspense? If you are the Messiah, tell us plainly."

Jesus answered, "I did tell you, but you do not believe. The works I do in my Father's name testify about Me, but you do not believe because you are not My sheep. My sheep listen to My voice; I know them, and they follow Me. I give them eternal life, and they shall never perish; no one will snatch them out of My hand. My Father, who has given them to Me, is greater than all; no one can snatch them out of My Father's hand. I and the Father are one." (NIV)

Prayer focus:

I come to You with an expectant heart during this festive season. You truly are the light of the universe and nothing can extinguish that light or Your love. Thank You for Your many miracles—even those that are yet to come. Thank you also for Your sustenance and provision. As I celebrate Your love this season, I think about how You came to earth as a baby boy, willing to embrace human form and even the cruelty of death on a cross in order that I might have eternal life. I am ever grateful that nothing can snatch me out of Your hand, even as You said! You are worthy of all my praise and I thank You for Your goodness and grace toward me. Amen.

ḦANUKKAH DAY 1

What is this holiday all about? Hanukkah originated during the period between the Old and New Testaments, probably 150 years or so before the birth of Christ. At that time, the land of Israel was occupied by the Syrians, following the rule of Alexander the Great. The Syrian ruler, Antiochus Epiphanes, wanted to abolish Jewish customs and laws, instead adopting much of the Greek culture that had been spread by Alexander. This included doing things that would have been considered abominable to Jews such as eating swine, not circumcising their males, worshiping Greek gods and many other things that went directly against God's laws. As attempts to assimilate Jews into the Greek culture increased, a resistance movement arose, led by rebels known as the Maccabees. Three years of struggle eventually led to victory and Jerusalem was reclaimed. On the twenty-fifth day of Kislev they offered sacrifices on the new altar which had been built and everyone worshiped the Lord.

This account is written in a book called *First Maccabees,* found in the *Apochrypha,* an ancient collection of writings that bridge the Old and New Testaments. While we do not consider these texts to be the inspired word of God, in this case they are considered a reliable historical source.

But there is more to the story! Tradition says that when the Jews were preparing to celebrate, there only a small amount of oil available to light the menorah, the candelabra used in the temple. It would take another eight days to prepare more oil, but by faith they lit the lamp. Even though there was only enough oil to last for one day, it lasted all eight days. This "miracle of Hanukkah" is a key element of the celebration, and explains why the menorah is lit for eight days in a row.

The second candle on the nine branched menorah is lit on this evening.

Scripture:

2 Samuel 22: 1–7; 13–31

David sang to the Lord the words of this song when the Lord delivered him from the hand of all his enemies and from the hand of Saul. He said:

"The Lord is my rock, my fortress and my deliverer;
my God is my rock, in whom I take refuge,
my shield and the horn of my salvation.
He is my stronghold, my refuge and my savior--
from violent people you save me.
"I called to the Lord, who is worthy of praise,
and have been saved from my enemies.
The waves of death swirled about me;
the torrents of destruction overwhelmed me.
The cords of the grave coiled around me;
the snares of death confronted me.
"In my distress I called to the Lord;
I called out to my God.

From His temple He heard my voice;
my cry came to His ears...

... Out of the brightness of His presence
bolts of lightning blazed forth.
The Lord thundered from heaven;
the voice of the Most High resounded.
He shot his arrows and scattered the enemy,
with great bolts of lightning He routed them.
The valleys of the sea were exposed
and the foundations of the earth laid bare
at the rebuke of the Lord,
at the blast of breath from His nostrils.
"He reached down from on high and took hold of me;
He drew me out of deep waters.
He rescued me from my powerful enemy,
from my foes, who were too strong for me.
They confronted me in the day of my disaster,
but the Lord was my support.
He brought me out into a spacious place;
He rescued me because He delighted in me.
"The Lord has dealt with me according to my right-
eousness;
according to the cleanness of my hands He has rewarded
me.
For I have kept the ways of the Lord;
I am not guilty of turning from my God.
All His laws are before me;
I have not turned away from His decrees.
I have been blameless before Him

and have kept myself from sin.
The Lord has rewarded me according to my righteousness,
according to my cleanness in His sight.
"To the faithful You show Yourself faithful,
to the blameless You show Yourself blameless,
to the pure You show Yourself pure,
but to the devious You show Yourself shrewd.
You save the humble,
but Your eyes are on the haughty to bring them low.
You, Lord, are my lamp;
the Lord turns my darkness into light.
With Your help I can advance against a troop;
with my God I can scale a wall.
"As for God, His way is perfect:
The Lord's word is flawless;
He shields all who take refuge in Him. (NIV)

Prayer focus:

Each day during Hanukkah, we will start by reciting a variation on the traditional blessing followed by a more personal prayer.

Blessed are You, Oh Lord our God, King of the Universe, who has set us apart as Your people, grafted into the blessings of Abraham, Isaac and Jacob. Blessed are You Oh Lord our God, King of the universe, who has done many miracles, both now and in the past. Blessed are You Oh Lord our God, King of the Universe, who has kept us in life, sustaining us, and who has given us joy as we celebrate Your coming.

You are a God of miracles and I can count on You to provide all that I need for sustenance, life, and joy. You will fight my battles! As I celebrate this holiday season with family and friends, may I be constantly reminded of Your goodness. During this Feast of Dedication, I rededicate my life to You. I dedicate everything that I am and all that I do; all that I hope and dream and love is Yours. May I be an ambassador for You, unapologetic in my faith and commitment to You, Oh God. I surrender every aspect of my life to You. May I be a shining example of Jesus to all I come in contact with.

ḤANUKKAH DAY 2

As mentioned yesterday, the supernatural significance of the oil lasting for all eight days is a key element of any Hanukkah celebration. It speaks to God's unfailing faithfulness in providing for His people. To commemorate the miracle of the oil, foods fried in oil are served during this season. For instance, fried doughnuts and latkes (potato pancakes) are popular dishes. However, oil is symbolic of more than just delicious food! In the Bible, oil is often used to symbolize the Holy Spirit. Even the golden lampstands themselves symbolize the Spirit of God. It is why the lamps in the temple were never to go out, for God's Holy Spirit is ever present, burning continually in our hearts and empowering us for His service.

On this evening, the third candle is lit.

Scripture:

Leviticus 24: 1–4

The Lord said to Moses, "Command the Israelites to bring you clear oil of pressed olives for the light so that the lamps may be kept burning continually. Outside the curtain that shields the ark of the covenant law in the tent of meeting, Aaron is to tend the lamps before the Lord from evening till morning, continually. This is to be a lasting ordinance for the generations to come. The lamps on the pure gold lampstand before the Lord must be tended continually. (NIV)

1 Corinthians 2: 4–14

My message and my preaching were not with wise and persuasive words, but with a demonstration of the Spirit's power, so that your faith might not rest on human wisdom, but on God's power.

We do, however, speak a message of wisdom among the mature, but not the wisdom of this age or of the rulers of this age, who are coming to nothing. No, we declare God's wisdom, a mystery that has been hidden and that God destined for our glory before time began. None of the rulers of this age understood it, for if they had, they would not have crucified the Lord of glory. However, as it is written:

"What no eye has seen, what no ear has heard, and what no human mind has conceived" the things God has prepared for those who love him--these are the things God has revealed to us by His Spirit.

The Spirit searches all things, even the deep things of God. For who knows a person's thoughts except their own spirit within them? In the same way no one knows the thoughts of God except the Spirit of God. What we have received is not the spirit of the world, but the Spirit who is from God, so that we may understand what God has freely given us. This is what we speak, not in words taught us by human wisdom but in words taught by the Spirit, explaining spiritual realities with Spirit-taught words. The person without the Spirit does not accept the things that come from the Spirit of God but considers them foolishness, and cannot understand them because they are discerned only through the Spirit. (NIV)

Prayer focus:

Blessed are You, Oh Lord our God, King of the Universe, who has set us apart for Your service. Blessed are You Oh Lord our God, King of the Universe, who has done great miracles. Blessed are You Oh Lord our God, King of the Universe, who has poured out Your Holy Spirit on those that believe.

I celebrate Your provision of oil, which represents Your Holy Spirit, Your healing and Your provision. Thank You for revealing to me the truth of the presence of Your Holy Spirit, which may seem like foolishness to the world, but which is the power of Christ in me! Even as You provided the miracle of the oil at Hanukkah, provide the oil of joy to my heart, through Jesus.

HANUKKAH DAY 3

Hanukkah is known as the "Festival of Lights" since so much emphasis is placed on lighting the candles each evening. We can't miss the connection between the burning lamp and Jesus who is the light of the world. He was heralded into the world with the bright light of the Bethlehem Star shining over the manger, and continues to light the way, even to this day.

Light the fourth candle this evening.

Scripture:

1 Corinthians 2: 4–14

Again Jesus spoke to them, saying, "I am the light of the world. Whoever follows me will not walk in darkness, but will have the light of life." (ESV)

John 9: 5

"While I am in the world, I am the Light of the world." (NASB)

Matthew 2: 1–12

Now after Jesus was born in Bethlehem of Judea in the days of Herod the king, behold, wise men from the east came to Jerusalem, saying, "Where is He who has been born king of the Jews? For we saw His star when it rose and have come to worship Him." When Herod the king heard this, he was troubled, and all Jerusalem with him; and assembling all the chief priests and scribes of the people, he inquired of them where the Christ was to be born. They told him, "In Bethlehem of Judea, for so it is written by the prophet:

"'And you, O Bethlehem, in the land of Judah, are by no means least among the rulers of Judah; for from you shall come a ruler who will shepherd my people Israel.'"

Then Herod summoned the wise men secretly and ascertained from them what time the star had appeared. And he sent them to Bethlehem, saying, "Go and search diligently for the child, and when you have found Him, bring me word, that I too may come and worship Him." After listening to the king, they went on their way. And behold, the star that they had seen when it rose went before them until it came to rest over the place where the child was. When they saw the star, they rejoiced exceedingly with great joy. And going into the house, they saw the child with Mary His mother, and they fell down and worshiped Him. Then, opening their treasures, they offered Him gifts, gold and frankincense and myrrh. And being warned in a dream not to return to Herod, they departed to their own country by another way. (ESV)

Prayer focus:

Blessed are You, Oh Lord our God, King of the Universe, who has set us apart for Your purposes. Blessed are You Oh Lord our God, King of the Universe, who has done great and mighty miracles. Blessed are You Oh Lord our God, King of the

Universe, who has given us new life, and who has brought us to this season to glorify You.

Jesus, You are the light of the world—even the entire universe! The light of Your lamp will never go out because You shine forever. Even the stars proclaim Your glory and majesty! You are the promised Messiah--Immanuel, Prince of Peace, Wonderful Counselor, King of Kings, Mighty One, Saviour, Redeemer and Friend; the Bright and Morning Star. As I continue to worship You during this festive season, may I never forget who You are and why You came to this earth.

HANUKKAH DAY 4

The story of Hanukkah contains a wonderful truth about God's unfailing mercy. Even in the midst of destruction and persecution, God will show His mercy to those that believe in Him. Besides the miracle of the oil, Jewish families also celebrate the victory represented by the Maccabee rebellion against tyranny. Parts of Daniel 11 are often read during Hanukkah because they contain prophecies that seemed to be fulfilled during the rule of Antiochus Epiphanes, the despicable leader who was in power during the events that led up to the Maccabee revolt. The prophecy talks about desecrating the temple and forsaking God's holy covenants. The 'abomination' may be the statue of Zeus that was erected in the temple. In any case, this passage, although not easy to understand, does bring to light that God is in control and that everything happens according to His 'appointed time.' We can take comfort in that fact and can rejoice that His mercy never fails.

The fifth candle is lit on this evening.

<u>Scripture:</u>

Daniel 11: 21–35

He will be succeeded by a contemptible person who has not been given the honor of royalty. He will invade the kingdom when its people feel secure, and he will seize it through intrigue. Then an overwhelming army will be swept away before him; both it and a prince of the covenant will be destroyed. After coming to an agreement with him, he will act deceitfully, and with only a few people he will rise to power. When the richest provinces feel secure, he will invade them and will achieve what neither his fathers nor his forefathers did. He will distribute plunder, loot and wealth among his followers. He will plot the overthrow of fortresses--but only for a time.

With a large army he will stir up his strength and courage against the king of the South. The king of the South will wage war with a large and very powerful army, but he will not be able to stand because of the plots devised against him. Those who eat from the king's provisions will try to destroy him; his army will be swept away, and many will fall in battle. The two kings, with their hearts bent on evil, will sit at the same table and lie to each other, but to no avail, because an end will still come at the appointed time. The king of the North will return to his own country with great wealth, but his heart will be set against the holy covenant. He will take action against it and then return to his own country.

At the appointed time he will invade the South again, but this time the outcome will be different from what it was before. Ships of the western coastlands will oppose him, and he will lose heart. Then he will turn back and vent his fury against the holy covenant. He will return and show favor to those who forsake the holy covenant.

His armed forces will rise up to desecrate the temple

fortress and will abolish the daily sacrifice. Then they will set up the abomination that causes desolation. With flattery he will corrupt those who have violated the covenant, but the people who know their God will firmly resist him.

Those who are wise will instruct many, though for a time they will fall by the sword or be burned or captured or plundered. When they fall, they will receive a little help, and many who are not sincere will join them. Some of the wise will stumble, so that they may be refined, purified and made spotless until the time of the end, for it will still come at the appointed time. (NIV)

Luke 1: 50

And His mercy is on them that fear Him from generation to generation. (KJV)

Romans 9: 22--24

What if God, desiring to show His wrath and to make known His power, has endured with much patience vessels of wrath prepared for destruction, in order to make known the riches of His glory for vessels of mercy, which He has prepared beforehand for glory--even us whom He has called, not from the Jews only but also from the Gentiles? (ESV)

Prayer focus:

Blessed are You, Oh Lord our God, King of the Universe, who has set us apart in order to make known the riches of Your glory. Blessed are You Oh Lord our God, King of the Universe, who has done great miracles in our midst. Blessed are You Oh Lord our God, King of the Universe, who has shown Your mercy to those You have called and have thrown off the oppressor at the appointed time.

I thank You for Your great mercy toward me, a sinner, undeserving of Your grace. Yet You chose me before the beginning of time and in the fulness of Your time, brought me into Your kingdom of light. I know I can trust You, for You are a God of patience and justice. I surrender my life into Your capable hands.

HANUKKAH DAY 5

One of the customs of many Jewish families during Hanukkah is playing a game using a dreidel, or a four sided top. On each of the four sides of the top is the initial of the letter for the message: "A Great Miracle Happened Here". To play the game, coins or candy are used as prizes. Each symbol or letter corresponds with an action: do nothing; take all; take half; add one to the pile. Each player starts by putting one item (coin or candy) into the 'pile'. Then, as each player takes a turn spinning the dreidel, they must do whatever action is spun. Each time the pile is emptied, everyone contributes another piece and the game continues until one player has all the pieces, or a time limit has been reached. Gifts are often also exchanged during Hanukkah, often one for each day of the festival. In any case, it is a time to have fun with family and friends, and to remember all God's blessings and miracles.

The sixth candle is lit on this evening.

Scripture:
Luke 18: 16

But Jesus called them to Him and said, "Let the little children come to Me, and do not forbid them; for of such is the kingdom of God. (NKJV)

Psalm 16:11

You will make known to me the path of life; In Your presence is fullness of joy; in Your right hand there are pleasures forever. (NASB)

Isaiah 55:12

For ye shall go out with joy, and be led forth with peace: the mountains and the hills shall break forth before you into singing, and all the trees of the field shall clap their hands. (KJV)

Prayer focus:

Blessed are You, Oh Lord our God, King of the Universe, who has set us apart for Your purposes. Blessed are You Oh Lord our God, King of the Universe, who has done miracles for our fathers in the days at this season. Blessed are You Oh Lord our God, King of the Universe, who has kept us in life, sustaining us, and who has brought us to this season.

I praise You today, Lord, and rejoice in Your goodness. Bless all the many gatherings of family and friends that are taking place this time of year. May each one be focused on You and Your goodness, and may we strive to keep the peace as we celebrate and have fun together. You delight in seeing Your children enjoying life, and so I gratefully embrace all that this season has to offer, keeping in mind that You, Jesus, are the reason for the season!

ḤANUKKAH DAY 6

Hanukkah spans the months of Kislev and Tevet, which starts tomorrow. It is a bridge that connects the months and allows for continued celebration of God's provision, mercy and miracles. The seventh candle is lit on this evening.

Since we are also very close to the beginning of the traditional new year according to western calendars, we can carry the light of Jesus into the next month and even into the next calendar year. Paul's prayer at the beginning of Colossians is a powerful way to pray for others, or ourselves, at this time. Simply insert your loved one's name (or your own name) into the prayer wherever the word 'you' appears.

Light the seventh candle!

Scripture:

Colossians 1: 3–14

We always thank God, the Father of our Lord Jesus Christ, when we pray for you, because we have heard of your faith in Christ Jesus and of the love you have for all God's people--the faith and love that spring from the hope stored up for you in heaven and about which you have already heard in the true message of the gospel that has come to you. In the same way, the gospel is bearing fruit and growing throughout the whole world--just as it has been doing among you since the day you heard it and truly understood God's grace. You learned it from Epaphras, our dear fellow servant, who is a faithful minister of Christ on our behalf, and who also told us of your love in the Spirit.

For this reason, since the day we heard about you, we have not stopped praying for you. We continually ask God to fill you with the knowledge of His will through all the wisdom and understanding that the Spirit gives, so that you may live a life worthy of the Lord and please Him in every way: bearing fruit in every good work, growing in the knowledge of God, being strengthened with all power according to His glorious might so that you may have great endurance and patience, and giving joyful thanks to the Father, who has qualified you to share in the inheritance of His holy people in the kingdom of light. For He has rescued us from the dominion of darkness and brought us into the kingdom of the Son He loves, in whom we have redemption, the forgiveness of sins. (NIV)

Deuteronomy 5: 32–33

So be careful to do what the Lord your God has commanded you; do not turn aside to the right or to the left. Walk in obedience to all that the Lord your God has commanded you, so that you may live and prosper and prolong your days in the land that you will possess. (NIV)

Prayer focus:

Blessed are You, Oh Lord our God, King of the Universe, who has set us apart for Your purposes. Blessed are You Oh

Lord our God, King of the Universe, who has done miracles for our forbearers and who continues to do miracles today. Blessed are You Oh Lord our God, King of the Universe, who has kept us in life, sustaining us, and who has brought us to this season and to the end of this month.

Lord, I pray the powerful words of the prayer from Colossians today over myself and over my loved ones. I dedicate each member of my family during this Feast of Dedication. Shine in our hearts this season and always. May You continue to guide me in Your truth in the coming months.

ḤANUKKAH DAY 7

It's a new month on the Jewish calendar! Today we celebrate a double blessing in that Hanukkah continues with the lighting of the eighth candle, but it is also a special day known as "Rosh Chodesh" or the "New Moon". The first of each month is set aside to honour the Lord with our "first fruits". This can include our time and our provisions.

One might wonder how Jewish people can afford so many "special" days throughout the year. We live in a busy world with many commitments and activities vying for our attention. How can we possibly set apart so many days to rest and reflect? There is the weekly Sabbath, the monthly new moon, plus all the special feast days. Does God really expect us to "do no ordinary work" so many times each year?

I think our answer lies in Paul's advice in his letters to the early church. We can never earn our salvation through doing good works, following traditions, or keeping a set schedule. We are no longer slaves to the law because Christ came as the fulfillment of that law. To *not* observe these special days does *not* affect our security in Christ.

However, there is blessing and joy in keeping His appointments because God honours His promises. Just like tithing doesn't make sense from a worldly point of view, God blesses us when we choose to tithe. So, too, our lives are enriched when we take time on His appointed days to reflect and worship Him. Somehow, He makes the remaining time more productive. Why not see for yourself this month?

Don't forget to light the eighth candle!

Scripture:

1 Corinthians 15: 20–28

But now Christ has been raised from the dead, the first fruits of those who are asleep. For since by a man came death, by a man also came the resurrection of the dead. For as in Adam all die, so also in Christ all will be made alive. But each in his own order: Christ the first fruits, after that those who are Christ's at His coming, then comes the end, when He hands over the kingdom to the God and Father, when He has abolished all rule and all authority and power. For He must reign until He has put all His enemies under His feet. The last enemy that will be abolished is death. For He has put all things in subjection under His feet. But when He says, "All things are put in subjection," it is evident that He is excepted who put all things in subjection to Him. When all things are subjected to Him, then the Son Himself also will be subjected to the One who subjected all things to Him, so that God may be all in all. (NASB)

Galatians 3: 10–14

For all who rely on works of the law are under a curse; for it is written, "Cursed be everyone who does not abide by all things written in the Book of the Law, and do them." Now it is evident that no one is justified before God by the law, for "The righteous shall live by faith." But the law is not of faith, rather "The one who does them shall live by them." Christ redeemed us from the curse of the law by becoming a curse for us--for it is written, "Cursed is everyone who is hanged on a tree"--so that in Christ Jesus the blessing of Abraham might come to the Gentiles, so that we might receive the promised Spirit through faith. (ESV)

Galatians 3: 21–29

Is the law then contrary to the promises of God? Certainly not! For if a law had been given that could give life, then righteousness would indeed be by the law. But the Scripture imprisoned everything under sin, so that the promise by faith in Jesus Christ might be given to those who believe.

Now before faith came, we were held captive under the law, imprisoned until the coming faith would be revealed. So then, the law was our guardian until Christ came, in order that we might be justified by faith. But now that faith has come, we are no longer under a guardian, for in Christ Jesus you are all sons of God, through faith. For as many of you as were baptized into Christ have put on Christ. There is neither Jew nor Greek, there is neither slave nor free, there is no male and female, for you are all one in Christ Jesus. And if you are Christ's, then you are Abraham's offspring, heirs according to promise. (ESV)

Romans 14: 5–8

One person esteems one day as better than another, while another esteems all days alike. Each one should be fully convinced in his own mind. The one who observes the day, observes it in honor of the Lord. The one who eats, eats in honor of the Lord, since he gives thanks to God, while the one who abstains, abstains in honor of the Lord and gives thanks to God. For none of us lives to himself, and none of us dies to himself. For if we live, we live to the Lord, and if we die, we die to the Lord. So then, whether we live or whether we die, we are the Lord's. (ESV)

Prayer focus:

Blessed are You, Oh Lord our God, King of the Universe, who has set us apart for Your purposes. Blessed are You Oh Lord our God, King of the Universe, who has done miracles for our fathers in the days at this season. Blessed are You Oh Lord our God, King of the Universe, who has kept us in life, sustaining us throughout the year.

Thank You for this special day and for another new month in which to worship You. I dedicate this month to You and pray for Your guidance and wisdom. Show me how I can honour You on Your appointed days without turning them into a burden or days filled with meaningless traditions. Instead, help me to worship You as You deserve. Continue to show me ways in which to dedicate the first fruits of my life to You.

HANUKKAH DAY 8

Today is the last day of Hanukkah! Since Hanukkah is known as the "Feast of Dedication" it seems like a good time to rededicate our lives to God. Also, Hanukkah is called the "Festival of Lights" stemming from the story of the menorah lights not going out, as we already read. The ninth and final candle is lit this evening, commemorating the miracle during the time of the Maccabees. It is the climax of the holiday and for many Jewish families the most important evening of the festival. Consider reviewing some of the traditions presented here and plan a celebration of your own. As Christians, we have added incentive to celebrate because we know Jesus will return to rule and reign!

Light that ninth candle!

Scripture:

Matthew 16: 24–28

Then Jesus told his disciples, "If anyone would come after me, let him deny himself and take up his cross and follow me. For whoever would save his life will lose it, but whoever loses his life for my sake will find it. For what will it profit a man if he gains the whole world and forfeits his soul? Or what shall a man give in return for his soul? For the Son of Man is going to come with his angels in the glory of his Father, and then he will repay each person according to what he has done. Truly, I say to you, there are some standing here who will not taste death until they see the Son of Man coming in his kingdom." (ESV)

Revelation 1: 4b—7

Grace to you and peace from Him who is and who was and who is to come, and from the seven spirits who are before His throne, and from Jesus Christ the faithful witness, the firstborn of the dead, and the ruler of kings on earth. To Him who loves us and has freed us from our sins by His blood and made us a kingdom, priests to His God and Father, to Him be glory and dominion forever and ever. Amen. Behold, He is coming with the clouds, and every eye will see Him, even those who pierced Him, and all tribes of the earth will wail on account of Him. Even so. Amen. (ESV)

Matthew 5: 14–19

"You are the light of the world. A city set on a hill cannot be hidden; nor does anyone light a lamp and put it under a basket, but on the lampstand, and it gives light to all who are in the house. Let your light shine before men in such a way that they may see your good works, and glorify your Father who is in heaven. Do not think that I came to abolish the Law or the Prophets; I did not come to abolish but to fulfill. For truly I say to you, until heaven and earth pass away, not the smallest letter or stroke shall pass from the Law until all is accomplished. Whoever then annuls one of the least of these commandments, and teaches others to do the same, shall be called least in the kingdom of heaven; but whoever keeps and teaches them, he shall be called great in the kingdom of heaven. (NASB)

<u>Prayer Focus:</u>

Blessed are You, Oh Lord our God, King of the Universe, who has set us apart for Your purposes. Blessed are You Oh Lord our God, King of the Universe, who has done miracles for our fathers in the days at this season. Blessed are You Oh Lord our God, King of the Universe, who has kept us in life, sustaining us, and who has brought us to this season.

I re-dedicate my life to You, Lord Jesus. You are the light of the world! You rule and reign in majesty over heaven and earth. Holy are You and worthy of all our praise. Worthy are You, the lamb that was slain. Holy, holy, holy is the Lord God Almighty. Blessing, strength and honour be to You, O Lord our God. You are King of Kings and Lord of Lords. The entire universe is Yours and by You all things were created. Thank You that You have reached down in Your mercy to commune with us. You are the light of the world, You shine like the sun, and Your glory never fades. You are our beacon of hope.

AFTERWORD

I hope you enjoyed this short book about celebrating Hanukkah. It is by no means meant to be exhaustive, nor it is meant to replace any other traditions you may already be enjoying. It is simply a suggested way to incorporate this lovely festival into the other traditions of the season, and to connect its celebration to the fulfillment of all things through Jesus. May you be blessed as you honour Him!

Blessed are You, Oh Lord our God, King of the Universe! Amen!

MORE IN THE SERIES

Hanukkah for Jesus Followers is an excerpt from a year long devotional series based on the Jewish calendar. All four seasons of *DIVINE APPOINTMENTS* are available in both paperback and hardcover. The set makes a wonderful gift.

If you enjoyed this book, please consider writing a review online. Reviews help readers find books they'll love and are tremendously helpful for today's authors. Thank you in advance!

Join Tracy's mailing list and get up to date info on all new releases, promos and giveaways when they happen. You'll also get a free book!

Visit Tracy's website for more titles including other devotional books, fiction and stage plays:

https://tracykrauss.com

ABOUT THE AUTHOR

Tracy Krauss is a multi-published novelist, playwright, and artist with several award winning and best selling novels, stage plays, devotionals and children's books in print. Her work strikes a chord with those looking for thought provoking faith based fiction laced with romance, suspense and humor. She holds a B.Ed from the University of Saskatchewan and has lived in many remote and interesting places in Canada's far north. She and her husband currently reside in beautiful Tumbler Ridge, BC where she continues to pursue all of her creative interests.

"Fiction on the edge – without crossing the line"
https://tracykrauss.com
or contact: tracy@tracykrauss.com